SPANISH PHRASES

SPANISH PHRASES

EASY SPANISH PHRASES FOR EVERYDAY LIFE

ANA COSTA ALONGI

SIGILLUM PUBLISHERS

TRACY, CALIFORNIA.

All rights reserved. No part of this publication may be reproduced, stored in a retrieval system or transmitted in any form, or by any means, electronic, mechanical, photocopying, recording, or otherwise without the prior written permission of the copyright holder, except brief quotations used
in a review.

Copyright © 2019 by SIGILLUM PUBLISHERS

ISBN 978-1-938898-15-0

Published by SIGILLUM PUBLISHERS
896 Lourence Dr. Tracy, California 95376

SigillumPublishers.com

First edition, January 2019.

Book cover and interior desing by Ana Alongi
AnaAlongi.com

Printed in the United States of America

Table of Content

Pronunciation	6
Basic Verbs	8
At a Meeting	11
At the Airport	13
At the Hotel	14
At the Coffee Shop	15
At the Doctor Office/ Emergency Room	17
Business	20
Courtesy and Protocol	22
Dining Out	24
Emergencies	26
Family	28
Money	29
Celebrations	30
Personal Feelings	31
Religion	32
Romance	33
For Students	36
For Teachers	38
Talking with Employees	39
Shopping	40
About the Author	42

PRONUNCIATION

To improve pronunciation, the sounds of letters must be read and learned. The phonetic symbols are not easy to understand, and most people don't comprehend them.

That is why the phonetics of the words are not included in this book. Instead, a guide for pronunciation has been added below. It is certainly more practical and comprehensible.

The sounds do not change when you pronounce the vowels. They are pronounced the same every time. Unlike the English language, the sounds are consistent.

Vocals

    A "ha" as in *apple*.

    E "eh" as in *end*.

    I "ee" as in *Indian*.

    O "oh" as in *odd*.

    U "oo" as in *food*.

Vowels

    B "b" as in *bold*.
    C "s" before e or i. Everywhere else it is pronounced as a soft "k".
    D "th" as in *domestic*.
    F "f" as in *farm*.
    G "h" before i or e. Everywhere else it is pronounced as a "g".
    H It is silent. Do not pronounce any sound. In foreign words (not Hispanic) is "g" as in *Hawai*.
    J "h" as in *hero*.
    K "k" as in *karate*.

L "l" as in *lama*.
LL "y" as in *jelly*.
M "m" as in *mom*.
N "n" as in *ninja*.
Ñ "ni" like the ni in *onion*.
P "p" as in *potato*.
Q "k" as in *quick*.
R "r" as in car. But at the beginning of a word or in between vowels is rolled.
S "s" as in *sound*.
T "d" as in *turquoise*.
V "b" as in *visa*.
W "w" as in *Washington*.
X "ks" as in *socks*.
Y "ee" if it is alone or at the end of a word. Otherwise "y" as in yes.
Z "s" as in *zebra*.

Combinations

GÜE and **GÜI:** the ü is pronounced as in bilingüe and pingüino.

GUE and **GUI:** the u is silent as in guerra, guitarra, guinda and guerrero.

CH: is "ch" as in cheese.

RR: strongly rolled. A little stronger than the "thr" in thriller.

BASIC VERBS

To be: Ser/Estar.
    Presente del Indicativo

> The verb to **be** can be translated in two different verbs in Spanish: **Ser** or **Estar**. The use of one verb or the other depends on the context.

Singular	
I am	Yo soy / Yo estoy
You are	Tú eres / Tú estás
He is	Él es / El está
She is	Ella es / Ella está
It is	Eso es / Eso está
Plural	
We are	Nosotros somos/ Nosotros estamos
You are	Vosotros sois/ Vosotros estáis
They are	Ellos son/ Ellos están

To have: Tener
    Presente del Indicativo

Singular	
I have	Yo tengo
You have	Tú tienes
He has	Él tiene
She has	Ella tiene
It has	Eso tiene
Plural	
We have	Nosotros tenemos
You have	Vosotros tenéis
They have	Ellos tienen

STARTING WITH THE BASICS

◆ My name is …
> *Mi nombre es …*

◆ What's your name?
> *¿Cómo te llamas?*

◆ Hello.
> *Hola.*

◆ Goodbye.
> *Adiós.*

◆ How are you?
> *¿Cómo estás?*

◆ I'm very well.
> *Estoy muy bien.*

◆ Thank you.
> *Gracias.*

◆ Mister…
> *Señor…*

◆ Mrs.
> *Señora.*

- Miss.
  Señorita.

- Good morning
  Buenos días.

- Good afternoon
  Buenas tardes.

- Good evening
  Buenas tardes.

- Good night
  Buenas noches.

AT A MEETING

❀ Nice to meet you.
Encantado de conocerte.

❀ I'm John.
Soy John.

❀ Hello, I'm …
Hola, soy …

❀ Pleased/nice to meet you.
Mucho gusto en conocerte.

❀ Welcome.
Bienvenido.

❀ Good morning.
Buenos días.

❀ Good afternoon.
Buenas tardes.

❀ Good evening.
Buenas noches.

❀ Good night.
Buenas noches.

❀ My name is …
Me llamo …

❈ Is the meeting here?
¿La reunión es aquí?

❈ The meeting is on Monday.
La reunión es el lunes.

❈ The meeting is canceled.
La reunión se ha cancelado.

❈ Where is the meeting?
¿Dónde es la reunión?

❈ When is the meeting?
¿Cuándo es la reunión?

❈ The meeting starts at 09:00 am.
La reunión comienza a las 9 am.

❈ See you later.
Nos vemos.

❈ See you tomorrow.
Hasta mañana.

❈ Have a nice day.
Que tenga un buen día.

❈ I hope to see you soon!
Espero verte pronto.

AT THE AIRPORT

❧ Where can I change money?
> *¿Dónde puedo cambiar dinero?*

❧ Where is the information desk?
> *¿Dónde está el mostrador de informes?*

❧ Where can I rent a car?
> *¿Dónde puedo rentar un auto?*

❧ Where is the train station?
> *¿Dónde está la estación de tren?*

❧ Where is Terminal A?
> *¿Dónde está la terminal A?*

❧ Where is Departures?
> *Dónde están las salidas.*

❧ Where is Arrivals?
> *¿Dónde están las llegadas?*

❧ I have luggage to dispatch.
> *Tengo equipaje para despachar.*

❧ This is my passport.
> *Este es mi pasaporte.*

❧ I would like to do a flight reservation.
> *Quiero hacer una reserva de avión.*

AT THE HOTEL

❀ I have a room booked.
>*Tengo una habitación reservada.*

❀ I need a non-smoking room.
>*Necesito un cuarto no fumador.*

❀ I do not smoke.
>*No fumo.*

❀ Can you wake me up at 8 am?
>*¿Puede despertarme a las 8 am?*

❀ I have a pet.
>*Tengo una mascota.*

❀ I'm leaving tomorrow.
>*Me voy mañana.*

❀ How much is the room for one night?
>*¿Cuánto cuesta el cuarto por una noche?*

❀ I would like to book a room.
>*Me gustaría reservar un cuarto.*

❀ How much do I owe you?
>*¿Cuánto le debo?*

AT THE COFFEE SHOP

◉ I would like...
> *Me gustaría...*

◉ A latte please.
> *Un café con leche por favor.*

◉ A coffee please.
> *Un café por favor.*

◉ A coffee and a croissant please.
> *Una café y un cruasán por favor.*

◉ A cappuccino please.
> *Un capuchino por favor.*

◉ A tea, please.
> *Un té por favor.*

◉ Give me that ...
> *Deme esa/e ...*

◉ Give me piece of cake please.
> *Deme una porción de torta por favor.*

◉ A big one.
> *Uno grande.*

◉ One medium.

Uno mediano.

◉ One small.

Uno chico.

◉ Can I have a glass of water please?

¿Me daría un vaso de agua por favor?

◉ How much is it?

¿Cuánto es la cuenta?

◉ It's to go.

Es para llevar.

◉ It is to eat here.

Es para comer aquí.

AT THE DOCTOR OFFICE/ EMERGENCY ROOM

◈ I need a doctor.
> *Necesito un médico.*

◈ I feel dizzy.
> *Me siento mareado.*

◈ I have a headache.
> *Me duele la cabeza.*

◈ My stomach hurts.
> *Me duele el estómago.*

◈ My chest hurts.
> *Me duele el pecho.*

◈ My right arm hurts.
> *Me duele el brazo derecho.*

◈ I find it hard to breathe.
> *Me cuesta respirar.*

◈ How much do you weigh?
> *¿Cuánto pesa?*

◈ I want to vomit.
> *Tengo ganas de vomitar.*

◈ I'm bleeding.
> *Estoy sangrando.*

- I vomited.

  He vomitado.

- I have diarrhea.

  Tengo diarrea.

- I have a fever.

  Tengo fiebre.

- I have good health.

  Tengo buena salud.

- I'm not in good health.

  No tengo buena salud.

- I need to do exercise.

  Necesito hacer exercisio.

- I want to lose weight.

  Quiero bajar de peso.

- I have overweight.

  Tengo sobrepeso.

- I have a wound in ...

  Tengo una herida en ...

- I've broken a bone.

  Me he roto un hueso.

- I fell.

  Me caí.

- Are you ok?

  ¿Estás bien?

- I feel very bad.

  Me siento muy mal.

- I'm not feeling well.

  No me siento bien.

- I feel better.

  Me siento mejor.

- Take care.

  Cuídate.

- I'm fine.

  Estoy bien.

BUSINESS

❋ He is your boss.
> *Él es tu jefe.*

❋ We'll sign the contract next week.
> *Vamos a firmar el contrato la semana que viene.*

❋ We have a deadline.
> *Tenemos una fecha límite.*

❋ Please sign here.
> *Por favor firme aquí.*

❋ We need your signature.
> *Necesitamos su firma.*

❋ I have very competitive prices.
> *Tengo precios muy competitivos.*

❋ Thank you for your purchase.
> *Gracias por su compra.*

❋ What is the price?
> *¿Cuánto sale?*

❋ It is on sale.
> *Está en oferta.*

❋ The price is…
> *El precio es…*

❃ Employees only.

Solo para empleados.

❃ We speak Spanish.

Se habla Español.

❃ Do not enter.

No entrar.

❃ Private area.

Privado.

COURTESY AND PROTOCOL

- Please.

  Por favor.

- You're welcome

  De nada.

- Thank you very much.

  Muchas gracias.

- Excuse me.

  Disculpe.

- Don't worry.

  No se preocupe.

- I'm sorry.

  Lo siento.

- May I …?

  ¿Puedo…?

- Absolutely!

  ¡Claro!

- Of course!

  ¡Por supuesto!

- Allow me.

  Permítame.

¿ No problem.
> *No hay problema.*

¿ Please take a seat.
> *Tome asiento por favor.*

¿ Nice to meet you.
> *Encantado de conocerlo.*

¿ It is a pleasure to meet you.
> *Es un placer conocerlo.*

¿ The pleasure is mine.
> *El placer es mío.*

¿ Come in please.
> *Adelante por favor.*

¿ Can I offer you something? (to drink or eat)
> *¿Le puedo ofrecer algo?*

¿ Do you want something to drink?
> *¿Quiere tomar algo?*

¿ It is an honor to meet you.
> *Es un honor conocerlo.*

¿ Merry Christmas
> *Feliz Navidad.*

¿ Happy New Year.
> *Feliz Año Nuevo.*

DINING OUT

❈ I would like a steak well done, please.
        Me gustaría un bife bien cocido, por favor.

❈ Medium rare, please.
        Término medio, por favor.

❈ Rare, please.
        Apenas cocido, por favor.

❈ This is cold.
        Esto está frío.

❈ The food is delicious.
        La comida es riquísima.

❈ I'm vegetarian.
        Soy vegetariano/a.

❈ Got anything gluten free?
        ¿Tiene algo sin gluten?

❈ Do you have anything low calories?
        ¿Tiene algo bajas calorias?

❈ Do you have anything sugar free?
        ¿Tiene algo sin azúcar?

❈ I have a reservation.
        Tengo una reservacion.

❂ A table for two, please.
> *Una mesa para dos por favor.*

❂ A table for four, please.
> *Una mesa para cuatro por favor.*

❂ Waiter, the menu please.
> *Mozo, el menú por favor.*

❂ Waiter, the check please.
> *Mozo, la adición por favor.*

❂ Do you have a wine list?
> *¿Tiene una carta de vinos?*

❂ Bring me the check, please.
> *Tráigame la cuenta, por favor.*

EMERGENCIES

◆ Someone follows me.
>*Alguien me sigue.*

◆ I've been robbed.
>*Me han robado.*

◆ Someone came into my house.
>*Alguien entro en mi casa.*

◆ I have been beaten.
>*Me han golpeado.*

◆ I had a car accident.
>*Tuve un accidente de auto.*

◆ My car has been stolen.
>*Me han robado el auto.*

◆ He is dead.
>*Está muerto.*

◆ She is dead.
>*Está muerta.*

◆ He/she does not breathe.
>*Él/Ella no respira.*

◆ He/she is unconscious.
>*Él/Ella está inconsciente.*

- Send an ambulance.
  > *Envíe una ambulacia.*

- I'm scared.
  > *Tengo miedo.*

- He/she is losing a lot of blood.
  > *Él/Ella está perdiendo mucha sangre.*

- I cannot donate blood.
  > *No puedo donar sangre.*

- Of course, I can donate blood.
  > *Por supuesto, puedo donar sangre.*

FAMILY

▹ This is my father.
> *Te presento a mi padre.*

▹ This is my mother.
> *Te presento a mi madre.*

▹ This is my wife.
> *Te presento a mi esposa.*

▹ This is my husband.
> *Te presento a mi esposo.*

▹ I have two sons.
> *Tengo dos hijos.*

▹ I'm a widow.
> *Soy viuda.*

▹ These are my kids/children.
> *Estos son mis niños.*

▹ I'm married.
> *Soy casado/a.*

▹ She is my daughter.
> *Ella es mi hija.*

▹ This is my son.
> *Este es mi hijo.*

MONEY

◉ Can you lend me money?
¿Me presta dinero?

◉ I have no money.
No tengo dinero.

◉ I can lend you money.
Puedo prestarte dinero.

◉ I have received my salary.
He cobrado mi sueldo.

◉ I've run out of money.
Me he quedado sin plata.

◉ I've made a lot of money.
He Ganado mucho dinero.

◉ I need money.
Me hace falta dinero.

◉ I do not have enough money.
No me alcanza el dinero.

◉ I need a raise.
Necesito un aumento de sueldo.

CELEBRATIONS

❀ Happy Birthday!

¡Feliz Cumpleaños!

❀ Happy Anniversary.

Feliz aniversario.

❀ Congratulations!

¡Lo felicito!

❀ Let's have a toast!

¡Brindemos!

❀ Chin-chin!

¡Chin Chin!

❀ Let's celebrate!

¡Celebremos!

❀ We have to celebrate!

¡Hay que celebrar!

❀ The party is tonight.

La fiesta es esta noche.

❀ Are you coming to the party?

¿Vienes a la fiesta?

❀ I'm celebrating the good news.

Estoy celebrando la buena noticia.

PERSONAL FEELINGS

❉ I'm happy.

> *Estoy contenta/content.*

❉ I'm sad.

> *Estoy triste.*

❉ I'm in a hurry.

> *Estoy apurada/apurado.*

❉ I'm nervous.

> *Estoy nerviosa/nervioso.*

❉ I'm hungry.

> *Tengo hambre.*

❉ I'm sleepy.

> *Tengo sueño.*

❉ I'm angry.

> *Estoy enojado.*

❉ I'm unhappy.

> *Soy infeliz.*

❉ How are you?

> *¿Cómo estás?*

❉ How do you feel?

> *¿Cómo te sientes?*

RELIGION

❀ I'm a Christian.
> **Soy Cristiana.**

❀ I'm an atheist.
> **Soy ateo.**

❀ I do not profess any religion.
> **No profeso ninguna religión.**

❀ I'm a very religious person.
> **Soy una persona muy religiosa.**

❀ I believe in God.
> **Creo en Dios.**

❀ I am not a religious person
> **No soy una persona religiosa.**

❀ I go to church.
> **Voy a la iglesia.**

❀ I'm doing a religious fasting.
> **Estoy haciendo un ayuno religioso.**

❀ My religion does not allow it.
> **Mi religión no me lo permite.**

❀ My religion forbids it.
> **Mi religión me lo prohibe.**

ROMANCE

- Can I see you again?
  > ¿*Puedo verte de nuevo?*

- I love you.
  > *Te amo.*

- I want to kiss you.
  > *Quiero besarte.*

- Kiss me.
  > *Bésame.*

- Do you want to go to the movies with me?
  > ¿*Quiere ir a ver una película conmigo?*

- You are beautiful.
  > *Eres hermosa (she)/ Eres hermoso (he).*

- What beautiful you are!
  > ¡*Que bella eres!*

- I love your eyes.
  > *Me encantan tus ojos.*

- These flowers are for you?
  > *Estas flores son para ti.*

- This is for you.
  > *Esto es para tí.*

- Will you marry me?
  ¿Aceptarías casarte conmigo?

- Will you be my wife?
  ¿Aceptarías ser mi esposa?

- My wife is the best.
  Mi esposa es de lo mejor.

- I love my husband.
  Amo a mi esposo.

- I'm married.
  Soy casado/ casada.

- I'm single.
  Soy soltero/ soltera.

- I'm gay.
  Soy gay.

- This is my boyfriend.
  Este es mi novio.

- This is my girlfriend.
  Esta es mi novia.

- I'm in love.
  Estoy enamorado.

- I'm in love with you.
  Estoy enamorado de ti.

- I'm falling for you.

    Me estoy enamorando de ti.

- I'm not jealous.

    No soy celoso.

- I'm jealous.

    Soy celoso.

- Come here.

    Ven aquí.

- Come with me.

    Ven conmigo.

- This is my fiance.

    Este es mi prometido.

- This is my fiancée.

    Esta es mi prometida.

FOR STUDENTS

◉ I'm late, please excuse me.
> *Llego tarde, disculpe.*

◉ I'm a student.
> *Soy un estudiante*

◉ I'm a graduate.
> *Soy un graduado.*

◉ I have a class.
> *Tengo clase.*

◉ I'm late for a clase.
> *Estoy llegando tarde a la clase.*

◉ I have good grades.
> *Tengo buenas calificaciones.*

◉ My professor is Mr...
> *Mi profesor es el señor...*

◉ Where should I go for my next class?
> *¿Dónde debo ir para mi siguiente clase?*

◉ I have an exam.
> *Tengo un examen.*

- I have to study.
   Tengo que estudiar.

- May I go to the restroom?
   ¿Puedo ir al baño?

- May I take this phone call?
   ¿Puedo contestar el teléfono?

- Can you repeat that in English/Spanish, please?
   ¿Puede repetir eso en ingles, por favor?

- I don't speak English/Spanish.
   No hablo inglés/español.

- The next class starts in 10 minutes.
   La siguiente clase comienza en 10 minutos.

- The first class is ELD (English Language Development)
   La primera clase es ELD (Desarrollo de la lengua Inglesa).

- I must go to see the counselor.
   Debo ir a ver al consejero/a.

- Where is the restroom?
   ¿Dónde está el baño?

- Where is the main office?
   ¿Dónde está la oficina principal?

FOR TEACHERS

- Good morning!

  ¡Buenos días!

- What is your name?

  ¿Cómo te llamas?

- Seat here, please.

  Sientate aquí, por favor.

- Put the phone away, please.

  Guarda el teléfono, por favor.

- Stop talking, please.

  Por favor no hablen.

- Do not use that language in class, Mr. ...

  No use ese lenguaje en clase, Señor ...

- Take out your notebooks.

  Saquen sus cuadernos.

- Take notes on your notebooks.

  Tomen notas en sus cuadernos.

- Open the books on page ...

  Abran el libro en la página ...

- Tomorrow I am going to start a new chapter.

  Mañana voy a comenzar un nuevo capítulo.

TALKING WITH EMPLOYEES

❁ You have done an excellent job.
> ***Usted ha hecho un excelente trabajo.***

❁ Wait a moment, please.
> ***Espere un momento por favor.***

❁ Please enter.
> ***Por favor entre.***

❁ Call Mr. ...
> ***Llame al Sr. ...***

❁ Close the door on exit.
> ***Cierre la puerta al salir.***

❁ You can begin.
> ***Puede comenzar.***

❁ You are a good employee.
> ***Usted es un buen empleado.***

❁ Best Employee Award.
> ***Premio al mejor empleado.***

❁ The employee of the week.
> ***El empleado de la semana.***

❁ Good job!
> ***¡Buen trabajo!***

SHOPPING

❈ How much is this?
¿Cuánto cuesta esto?

❈ May I try this?
¿Me podría probar esto?

❈ Can I pay with a credit card?
¿Puedo pagar con tarjeta de crédito?

❈ I pay with credit card.
Pago con tarjeta de crédito.

❈ Do you pay with cash?
¿Paga con efectivo?

❈ I pay with cash.
Pago con efectivo.

❈ Do you accept credit cards?
¿Acepta tarjeta de crédito?

❈ I want to return this merchandise.
Quiero devolver esta mercadería.

❈ Where is the fitting room?
¿Dónde está el probador?

❈ Smoking is allowed?
¿Se permite fumar?

❀ What time does the store close?
>*¿A que hora cierra el negocio?*

❀ What time does the store open?
>*¿A que hora abre el negocio?*

❀ Do you speak English?
>*¿Habla usted Inglés?*

❀ Do you have a smaller size?
>*¿Tiene una talla más pequeña?*

❀ Do you have a bigger size?
>*¿Tiene una talla más grande?*

❀ Do you have these pants in other colors?
>*¿Tiene este pantalón en otros colores?*

❀ What is the discount?
>*¿Cuál es el descuento?*

❀ I am going to buy these items.
>*Voy a comprar estos artículos.*

ABOUT THE AUTHOR

Ana Costa Alongi was born in the year 1960 in Buenos Aires, Argentina. She is a Spanish editor, writer, graphic artist, publisher, and educator.

The author is a very spiritual person. Beginning in 1988 as a religious worker, she has educated and improved the lives of people in four countries, Argentina, Venezuela, Mexico, and the United States. Her extensive experience in education also includes the public school where she works as a trilingual educator since French is another language in which she is fluent.

Ana's career as an author began as a novelist. She won several awards for her saga The Chronicles of Time and for this reason, she was invited and serves as Judge in the international literary contest Dan Poynter's Global Ebook Awards. As an editor of the Spanish language, she has contributed as a consultant to the IBPA (Independent Book Publishers Association).

At present Ana resides in California and is working on the saga The Chronicles of Time. The titles already published in this series are Cuerpo Mortal (Book 1) and Alma Inmortal (Book 2).

Cuerpo Mortal has won five international literary awards and has been translated into English under the title Mortal Flesh, The Last Hero of Pompeii.

Cuerpo Mortal, the Spanish edition, was awarded:
- Best Fantasy 2012, first place, Global Ebook Awards
- The Mariposa Award 2013, second place, International Latino Book Awards.
- Honorable Mention in Romance 2012, Global Ebook Awards

Mortal Flesh, the English edition, was awarded:
- Best fantasy / Sci-fi 2013, first place, Latino Books into Movies Awards.
- Best fantasy / Sci-fi 2013, second place, International Latino Book Awards

Alma Immortal has been translated into English under the title Immortal Soul and has won two international literary awards:
- Best fantasy / contemporary 2013, Gold medal, Global Ebook Awards
- Fantasy / History setting 2013, Gold medal, Global Ebook Awards

Ana is writing the third book of the saga.

www.ingramcontent.com/pod-product-compliance
Lightning Source LLC
Chambersburg PA
CBHW061310040426
42444CB00010B/2577